Deam Journal

Date:_____   Time:_____

Thoughts Before Sleep

_____
_____
_____
_____
_____

Emotions Before Sleep

_____

Dream

_____
_____
_____
_____
_____
_____
_____

Interpretation

_____
_____

Feeling Upon Awakening

_____
_____
_____

Comments

_____
_____
_____

Deam Journal

Date:_____   Time:_____

Thoughts Before Sleep

_____
_____
_____
_____
_____

Emotions Before Sleep

_____

Dream

_____
_____
_____
_____
_____
_____

Interpretation

_____
_____
_____

Feeling Upon Awakening

_____
_____
_____

Comments

_____
_____

Deam Journal

Date:_____   Time:_____

Thoughts Before Sleep

_____
_____
_____
_____
_____

Emotions Before Sleep

_____

Dream

_____
_____
_____
_____
_____
_____
_____
_____

Interpretation

_____
_____
_____

Feeling Upon Awakening

_____
_____
_____

Comments

_____
_____
_____

Deam Journal

Date:_____   Time:_____

Thoughts Before Sleep

_____
_____
_____
_____
_____

Emotions Before Sleep

_____

Dream

_____
_____
_____
_____
_____
_____
_____
_____

Interpretation

_____
_____
_____

Feeling Upon Awakening

_____
_____
_____

Comments

_____
_____
_____

Dream Journal

Date:_____   Time:_____

Thoughts Before Sleep

_____

_____

_____

_____

_____

Emotions Before Sleep

_____

Dream

_____

_____

_____

_____

_____

_____

_____

Interpretation

_____

_____

Feeling Upon Awakening

_____

_____

_____

Comments

_____

_____

_____

Deam Journal

Date:_____ Time:_____

Thoughts Before Sleep

_____
_____
_____
_____
_____

Emotions Before Sleep

_____

Dream

_____
_____
_____
_____
_____
_____

Interpretation

_____
_____

Feeling Upon Awakening

_____
_____
_____

Comments

_____
_____
_____

Deam Journal

Date:_____   Time:_____

Thoughts Before Sleep

_____
_____
_____
_____
_____

Emotions Before Sleep

_____

Dream

_____
_____
_____
_____
_____
_____
_____
_____

Interpretation

_____
_____
_____

Feeling Upon Awakening

_____
_____
_____

Comments

_____
_____
_____

Deam Journal

Date:_____   Time:_____

Thoughts Before Sleep

_____

_____

_____

_____

_____

Emotions Before Sleep

_____

Dream

_____

_____

_____

_____

_____

_____

_____

Interpretation

_____

_____

Feeling Upon Awakening

_____

_____

_____

Comments

_____

_____

Deam Journal

Date:_____   Time:_____

Thoughts Before Sleep

_____
_____
_____
_____
_____

Emotions Before Sleep

_____

Dream

_____
_____
_____
_____
_____
_____
_____

Interpretation

_____
_____
_____

Feeling Upon Awakening

_____
_____
_____

Comments

_____
_____
_____

Dream Journal

Date:_____   Time:_____

Thoughts Before Sleep

_____
_____
_____
_____
_____

Emotions Before Sleep

_____

Dream

_____
_____
_____
_____
_____
_____
_____

Interpretation

_____
_____

Feeling Upon Awakening

_____
_____
_____

Comments

_____
_____
_____

Deam Journal

Date:_____   Time:_____

Thoughts Before Sleep

_____
_____
_____
_____
_____

Emotions Before Sleep

_____

Dream

_____
_____
_____
_____
_____
_____
_____

Interpretation

_____
_____

Feeling Upon Awakening

_____
_____
_____

Comments

_____
_____
_____

Deam Journal

Date:_____   Time:_____

Thoughts Before Sleep

_____
_____
_____
_____
_____

Emotions Before Sleep

_____

Dream

_____
_____
_____
_____
_____
_____
_____

Interpretation

_____
_____
_____

Feeling Upon Awakening

_____
_____
_____

Comments

_____
_____
_____

Deam Journal

Date:_____   Time:_____

Thoughts Before Sleep

_____
_____
_____
_____
_____

Emotions Before Sleep

_____

Dream

_____
_____
_____
_____
_____
_____
_____

Interpretation

_____
_____
_____

Feeling Upon Awakening

_____
_____
_____

Comments

_____
_____
_____

Deam Journal

Date:_____   Time:_____

Thoughts Before Sleep

_____
_____
_____
_____
_____

Emotions Before Sleep

_____

Dream

_____
_____
_____
_____
_____
_____
_____

Interpretation

_____
_____
_____

Feeling Upon Awakening

_____
_____
_____

Comments

_____
_____
_____

Deam Journal

Date:_____   Time:_____

Thoughts Before Sleep

_____
_____
_____
_____
_____

Emotions Before Sleep

_____

Dream

_____
_____
_____
_____
_____
_____
_____

Interpretation

_____
_____

Feeling Upon Awakening

_____
_____
_____

Comments

_____
_____
_____

Deam Journal

Date:_____   Time:_____

Thoughts Before Sleep

Emotions Before Sleep

Dream

Interpretation

Feeling Upon Awakening

Comments

Dream Journal

Date:_____   Time:_____

Thoughts Before Sleep

_____
_____
_____
_____
_____

Emotions Before Sleep

_____

Dream

_____
_____
_____
_____
_____
_____
_____
_____

Interpretation

_____
_____
_____

Feeling Upon Awakening

_____
_____
_____

Comments

_____
_____
_____

Deam Journal

Date:_____   Time:_____

Thoughts Before Sleep

Emotions Before Sleep

Dream

Interpretation

Feeling Upon Awakening

Comments

Deam Journal

Date:_____   Time:_____

Thoughts Before Sleep

_____
_____
_____
_____

Emotions Before Sleep

_____

Dream

_____
_____
_____
_____
_____
_____
_____

Interpretation

_____
_____
_____

Feeling Upon Awakening

_____
_____
_____

Comments

_____
_____
_____

Deam Journal

Date:_____   Time:_____

Thoughts Before Sleep

_____

_____

_____

_____

Emotions Before Sleep

_____

Dream

_____

_____

_____

_____

_____

_____

Interpretation

_____

_____

Feeling Upon Awakening

_____

_____

_____

Comments

_____

_____

Deam Journal

Date:_____   Time:_____

Thoughts Before Sleep

_____
_____
_____
_____
_____
_____

Emotions Before Sleep

_____

Dream

_____
_____
_____
_____
_____
_____
_____
_____
_____

Interpretation

_____
_____
_____

Feeling Upon Awakening

_____
_____
_____

Comments

_____
_____
_____

Deam Journal

Date:_____ Time:_____

Thoughts Before Sleep

Emotions Before Sleep

Dream

Interpretation

Feeling Upon Awakening

Comments

Deam Journal

Date:_____   Time:_____

Thoughts Before Sleep

_____
_____
_____
_____
_____

Emotions Before Sleep

_____

Dream

_____
_____
_____
_____
_____
_____
_____
_____

Interpretation

_____
_____
_____

Feeling Upon Awakening

_____
_____
_____

Comments

_____
_____
_____

Deam Journal

Date:_____   Time:_____

Thoughts Before Sleep

_____
_____
_____
_____
_____

Emotions Before Sleep

_____

Dream

_____
_____
_____
_____
_____
_____
_____

Interpretation

_____
_____
_____

Feeling Upon Awakening

_____
_____
_____

Comments

_____
_____

Deam Journal

Date:_____   Time:_____

Thoughts Before Sleep

Emotions Before Sleep

Dream

Interpretation

Feeling Upon Awakening

Comments

Deam Journal

Date:_____   Time:_____

Thoughts Before Sleep

Emotions Before Sleep

Dream

Interpretation

Feeling Upon Awakening

Comments

Deam Journal

Date:_____ Time:_____

Thoughts Before Sleep

_____
_____
_____
_____
_____

Emotions Before Sleep

_____

Dream

_____
_____
_____
_____
_____
_____
_____
_____

Interpretation

_____
_____
_____

Feeling Upon Awakening

_____
_____
_____

Comments

_____
_____
_____

Deam Journal

Date:_____   Time:_____

Thoughts Before Sleep

_____
_____
_____
_____
_____

Emotions Before Sleep

_____

Dream

_____
_____
_____
_____
_____
_____
_____

Interpretation

_____
_____
_____

Feeling Upon Awakening

_____
_____
_____

Comments

_____
_____

Deam Journal

Date:_____ Time:_____

Thoughts Before Sleep

_____
_____
_____
_____
_____

Emotions Before Sleep

_____

Dream

_____
_____
_____
_____
_____
_____

Interpretation

_____
_____

Feeling Upon Awakening

_____
_____
_____

Comments

_____
_____
_____

Deam Journal

Date:_____   Time:_____

Thoughts Before Sleep

_____
_____
_____
_____
_____

Emotions Before Sleep

_____

Dream

_____
_____
_____
_____
_____
_____
_____

Interpretation

_____
_____

Feeling Upon Awakening

_____
_____
_____

Comments

_____
_____

Deam Journal

Date:_____   Time:_____

Thoughts Before Sleep

_____
_____
_____
_____
_____

Emotions Before Sleep

_____

Dream

_____
_____
_____
_____
_____
_____
_____

Interpretation

_____
_____
_____

Feeling Upon Awakening

_____
_____
_____

Comments

_____
_____
_____

Deam Journal

Date:_____   Time:_____

Thoughts Before Sleep

Emotions Before Sleep

Dream

Interpretation

Feeling Upon Awakening

Comments

Deam Journal

Date:_____   Time:_____

Thoughts Before Sleep

_____
_____
_____
_____
_____

Emotions Before Sleep

_____

Dream

_____
_____
_____
_____
_____
_____
_____

Interpretation

_____
_____

Feeling Upon Awakening

_____
_____

Comments

_____
_____
_____

Deam Journal

Date:_____   Time:_____

Thoughts Before Sleep

Emotions Before Sleep

Dream

Interpretation

Feeling Upon Awakening

Comments

Deam Journal

Date:_____   Time:_____

Thoughts Before Sleep

_____
_____
_____
_____
_____

Emotions Before Sleep

_____

Dream

_____
_____
_____
_____
_____
_____
_____

Interpretation

_____
_____
_____

Feeling Upon Awakening

_____
_____
_____

Comments

_____
_____
_____

Deam Journal

Date:_____   Time:_____

Thoughts Before Sleep

Emotions Before Sleep

Dream

Interpretation

Feeling Upon Awakening

Comments

Dream Journal

Date:_____   Time:_____

Thoughts Before Sleep

Emotions Before Sleep

Dream

Interpretation

Feeling Upon Awakening

Comments

Deam Journal

Date:_____   Time:_____

Thoughts Before Sleep

_____
_____
_____
_____
_____

Emotions Before Sleep

_____

Dream

_____
_____
_____
_____
_____
_____
_____

Interpretation

_____
_____

Feeling Upon Awakening

_____
_____
_____

Comments

_____
_____

Deam Journal

Date:_____   Time:_____

Thoughts Before Sleep

_____
_____
_____
_____
_____
_____

Emotions Before Sleep

_____

Dream

_____
_____
_____
_____
_____
_____
_____
_____

Interpretation

_____
_____
_____

Feeling Upon Awakening

_____
_____
_____

Comments

_____
_____
_____

Deam Journal

Date:_____   Time:_____

Thoughts Before Sleep

_____
_____
_____
_____
_____

Emotions Before Sleep

_____

Dream

_____
_____
_____
_____
_____
_____
_____

Interpretation

_____
_____

Feeling Upon Awakening

_____
_____
_____

Comments

_____
_____

Dream Journal

Date:_____   Time:_____

Thoughts Before Sleep

_____
_____
_____
_____
_____

Emotions Before Sleep

_____

Dream

_____
_____
_____
_____
_____
_____
_____

Interpretation

_____
_____
_____

Feeling Upon Awakening

_____
_____
_____

Comments

_____
_____
_____

Deam Journal

Date:_____   Time:_____

Thoughts Before Sleep

_____
_____
_____
_____
_____

Emotions Before Sleep

_____

Dream

_____
_____
_____
_____
_____
_____
_____

Interpretation

_____
_____
_____

Feeling Upon Awakening

_____
_____
_____

Comments

_____
_____
_____

Deam Journal

Date:_____   Time:_____

Thoughts Before Sleep

_____
_____
_____
_____

Emotions Before Sleep

_____

Dream

_____
_____
_____
_____
_____
_____
_____

Interpretation

_____
_____
_____

Feeling Upon Awakening

_____
_____
_____

Comments

_____
_____
_____

Deam Journal

Date:_____ Time:_____

Thoughts Before Sleep

Emotions Before Sleep

Dream

Interpretation

Feeling Upon Awakening

Comments

Dream Journal

Date:_____   Time:_____

Thoughts Before Sleep

_____
_____
_____
_____
_____

Emotions Before Sleep

_____

Dream

_____
_____
_____
_____
_____
_____
_____

Interpretation

_____
_____
_____

Feeling Upon Awakening

_____
_____
_____

Comments

_____
_____
_____

Dream Journal

Date:_____   Time:_____

Thoughts Before Sleep

Emotions Before Sleep

Dream

Interpretation

Feeling Upon Awakening

Comments

Deam Journal

Date:_____   Time:_____

Thoughts Before Sleep

_____
_____
_____
_____
_____

Emotions Before Sleep

_____

Dream

_____
_____
_____
_____
_____
_____
_____
_____

Interpretation

_____
_____
_____

Feeling Upon Awakening

_____
_____
_____

Comments

_____
_____
_____

Deam Journal

Date:_____ Time:_____

Thoughts Before Sleep

_____
_____
_____
_____
_____

Emotions Before Sleep

_____

Dream

_____
_____
_____
_____
_____
_____
_____

Interpretation

_____
_____
_____

Feeling Upon Awakening

_____
_____
_____

Comments

_____
_____
_____

Deam Journal

Date:_____   Time:_____

Thoughts Before Sleep

_____
_____
_____
_____
_____

Emotions Before Sleep

_____

Dream

_____
_____
_____
_____
_____
_____
_____

Interpretation

_____
_____

Feeling Upon Awakening

_____
_____
_____

Comments

_____
_____
_____

Deam Journal

Date:_____ Time:_____

Thoughts Before Sleep

_____
_____
_____
_____
_____

Emotions Before Sleep

_____

Dream

_____
_____
_____
_____
_____
_____
_____

Interpretation

_____
_____
_____

Feeling Upon Awakening

_____
_____
_____

Comments

_____
_____
_____

Dream Journal

Date:_____   Time:_____

Thoughts Before Sleep

_____
_____
_____
_____
_____

Emotions Before Sleep

_____

Dream

_____
_____
_____
_____
_____
_____
_____

Interpretation

_____
_____
_____

Feeling Upon Awakening

_____
_____
_____

Comments

_____
_____
_____

Deam Journal

Date:_____   Time:_____

Thoughts Before Sleep

_____
_____
_____
_____
_____

Emotions Before Sleep

_____

Dream

_____
_____
_____
_____
_____
_____
_____

Interpretation

_____
_____

Feeling Upon Awakening

_____
_____
_____

Comments

_____
_____

Deam Journal

Date:_____   Time:_____

Thoughts Before Sleep

_____
_____
_____
_____
_____

Emotions Before Sleep

_____

Dream

_____
_____
_____
_____
_____
_____
_____

Interpretation

_____
_____

Feeling Upon Awakening

_____
_____
_____

Comments

_____
_____
_____

Deam Journal

Date:_____   Time:_____

Thoughts Before Sleep

_____
_____
_____
_____
_____

Emotions Before Sleep

_____

Dream

_____
_____
_____
_____
_____
_____
_____

Interpretation

_____
_____

Feeling Upon Awakening

_____
_____
_____

Comments

_____
_____

Deam Journal

Date:_____   Time:_____

Thoughts Before Sleep

_____
_____
_____
_____
_____

Emotions Before Sleep

_____

Dream

_____
_____
_____
_____
_____
_____
_____

Interpretation

_____
_____

Feeling Upon Awakening

_____
_____
_____

Comments

_____
_____
_____

Deam Journal

Date:_____   Time:_____

Thoughts Before Sleep

Emotions Before Sleep

Dream

Interpretation

Feeling Upon Awakening

Comments

Deam Journal

Date:_____   Time:_____

Thoughts Before Sleep

_____
_____
_____
_____
_____

Emotions Before Sleep

_____

Dream

_____
_____
_____
_____
_____
_____
_____

Interpretation

_____
_____

Feeling Upon Awakening

_____
_____
_____

Comments

_____
_____
_____

Deam Journal

Date:_____   Time:_____

Thoughts Before Sleep

_____
_____
_____
_____
_____

Emotions Before Sleep

_____

Dream

_____
_____
_____
_____
_____
_____
_____

Interpretation

_____
_____
_____

Feeling Upon Awakening

_____
_____
_____

Comments

_____
_____
_____

Deam Journal

Date:_____ Time:_____

Thoughts Before Sleep

_____
_____
_____
_____
_____

Emotions Before Sleep

_____

Dream

_____
_____
_____
_____
_____
_____
_____

Interpretation

_____
_____
_____

Feeling Upon Awakening

_____
_____
_____

Comments

_____
_____
_____

Dream Journal

Date:_____   Time:_____

Thoughts Before Sleep

_____
_____
_____
_____
_____

Emotions Before Sleep

_____

Dream

_____
_____
_____
_____
_____
_____
_____
_____

Interpretation

_____
_____

Feeling Upon Awakening

_____
_____
_____

Comments

_____
_____

Deam Journal

Date:_____   Time:_____

Thoughts Before Sleep

_____
_____
_____
_____
_____

Emotions Before Sleep

_____

Dream

_____
_____
_____
_____
_____
_____
_____
_____

Interpretation

_____
_____
_____

Feeling Upon Awakening

_____
_____
_____

Comments

_____
_____
_____

Deam Journal

Date:_____ Time:_____

Thoughts Before Sleep

_____
_____
_____
_____
_____

Emotions Before Sleep

_____

Dream

_____
_____
_____
_____
_____
_____
_____

Interpretation

_____
_____
_____

Feeling Upon Awakening

_____
_____
_____

Comments

_____
_____
_____

Deam Journal

Date:_____   Time:_____

Thoughts Before Sleep

_____
_____
_____
_____
_____

Emotions Before Sleep

_____

Dream

_____
_____
_____
_____
_____
_____
_____

Interpretation

_____
_____
_____

Feeling Upon Awakening

_____
_____
_____

Comments

_____
_____
_____

Dream Journal

Date:_____ Time:_____

Thoughts Before Sleep

_____
_____
_____
_____
_____

Emotions Before Sleep

_____

Dream

_____
_____
_____
_____
_____
_____
_____
_____

Interpretation

_____
_____

Feeling Upon Awakening

_____
_____
_____

Comments

_____
_____

Deam Journal

Date:_____   Time:_____

Thoughts Before Sleep

_____
_____
_____
_____
_____

Emotions Before Sleep

_____

Dream

_____
_____
_____
_____
_____
_____
_____

Interpretation

_____
_____

Feeling Upon Awakening

_____
_____
_____

Comments

_____
_____
_____

Deam Journal

Date:_____   Time:_____

Thoughts Before Sleep

Emotions Before Sleep

Dream

Interpretation

Feeling Upon Awakening

Comments

Deam Journal

Date:_____   Time:_____

Thoughts Before Sleep

_____
_____
_____
_____
_____

Emotions Before Sleep

_____

Dream

_____
_____
_____
_____
_____
_____
_____
_____

Interpretation

_____
_____

Feeling Upon Awakening

_____
_____
_____

Comments

_____
_____
_____

Dream Journal

Date:_____ Time:_____

Thoughts Before Sleep

Emotions Before Sleep

Dream

Interpretation

Feeling Upon Awakening

Comments

Dream Journal

Date:_____ Time:_____

Thoughts Before Sleep

Emotions Before Sleep

Dream

Interpretation

Feeling Upon Awakening

Comments

Dream Journal

Date:_____   Time:_____

Thoughts Before Sleep

Emotions Before Sleep

Dream

Interpretation

Feeling Upon Awakening

Comments

Deam Journal

Date:_____   Time:_____

Thoughts Before Sleep

_____
_____
_____
_____
_____

Emotions Before Sleep

_____

Dream

_____
_____
_____
_____
_____
_____
_____

Interpretation

_____
_____

Feeling Upon Awakening

_____
_____
_____

Comments

_____
_____
_____

Deam Journal

Date:_____   Time:_____

Thoughts Before Sleep

_____
_____
_____
_____
_____

Emotions Before Sleep

_____

Dream

_____
_____
_____
_____
_____
_____
_____

Interpretation

_____
_____
_____

Feeling Upon Awakening

_____
_____
_____

Comments

_____
_____

Deam Journal

Date:_____ Time:_____

Thoughts Before Sleep

_____
_____
_____
_____
_____

Emotions Before Sleep

_____

Dream

_____
_____
_____
_____
_____
_____
_____
_____

Interpretation

_____
_____
_____

Feeling Upon Awakening

_____
_____
_____

Comments

_____
_____
_____

Deam Journal

Date:_____   Time:_____

Thoughts Before Sleep

_____
_____
_____
_____
_____

Emotions Before Sleep

_____

Dream

_____
_____
_____
_____
_____
_____
_____

Interpretation

_____
_____

Feeling Upon Awakening

_____
_____
_____

Comments

_____
_____

Deam Journal

Date:_____   Time:_____

Thoughts Before Sleep

_____
_____
_____
_____
_____

Emotions Before Sleep

_____

Dream

_____
_____
_____
_____
_____
_____
_____

Interpretation

_____
_____

Feeling Upon Awakening

_____
_____
_____

Comments

_____
_____
_____

Dream Journal

Date:_____   Time:_____

Thoughts Before Sleep

_____
_____
_____
_____
_____

Emotions Before Sleep

_____

Dream

_____
_____
_____
_____
_____
_____
_____

Interpretation

_____
_____

Feeling Upon Awakening

_____
_____
_____

Comments

_____
_____

Deam Journal

Date:_____   Time:_____

Thoughts Before Sleep

_____
_____
_____
_____
_____

Emotions Before Sleep

_____

Dream

_____
_____
_____
_____
_____
_____
_____

Interpretation

_____
_____
_____

Feeling Upon Awakening

_____
_____
_____

Comments

_____
_____
_____

Dream Journal

Date:_____   Time:_____

Thoughts Before Sleep

_____
_____
_____
_____
_____

Emotions Before Sleep

_____

Dream

_____
_____
_____
_____
_____
_____
_____

Interpretation

_____
_____

Feeling Upon Awakening

_____
_____
_____

Comments

_____
_____
_____

Deam Journal

Date:_____   Time:_____

Thoughts Before Sleep

_____
_____
_____
_____
_____

Emotions Before Sleep

_____

Dream

_____
_____
_____
_____
_____
_____
_____

Interpretation

_____
_____

Feeling Upon Awakening

_____
_____
_____

Comments

_____
_____
_____

Deam Journal

Date:_____   Time:_____

Thoughts Before Sleep

_____
_____
_____
_____
_____

Emotions Before Sleep

_____

Dream

_____
_____
_____
_____
_____
_____
_____

Interpretation

_____
_____

Feeling Upon Awakening

_____
_____
_____

Comments

_____
_____

Deam Journal

Date:_____   Time:_____

Thoughts Before Sleep

_____
_____
_____
_____
_____

Emotions Before Sleep

_____

Dream

_____
_____
_____
_____
_____
_____
_____
_____

Interpretation

_____
_____
_____

Feeling Upon Awakening

_____
_____
_____

Comments

_____
_____
_____

Dream Journal

Date:_____ Time:_____

Thoughts Before Sleep

_____
_____
_____
_____
_____

Emotions Before Sleep

_____

Dream

_____
_____
_____
_____
_____
_____
_____

Interpretation

_____
_____

Feeling Upon Awakening

_____
_____
_____

Comments

_____
_____
_____

Deam Journal

Date:_____   Time:_____

Thoughts Before Sleep

_____
_____
_____
_____
_____

Emotions Before Sleep

_____

Dream

_____
_____
_____
_____
_____
_____
_____

Interpretation

_____
_____
_____

Feeling Upon Awakening

_____
_____
_____

Comments

_____
_____
_____

Dream Journal

Date:_____   Time:_____

Thoughts Before Sleep

_____
_____
_____
_____
_____

Emotions Before Sleep

_____

Dream

_____
_____
_____
_____
_____
_____
_____
_____

Interpretation

_____
_____
_____

Feeling Upon Awakening

_____
_____
_____

Comments

_____
_____
_____

Deam Journal

Date:_____ Time:_____

Thoughts Before Sleep

_____
_____
_____
_____
_____

Emotions Before Sleep

_____

Dream

_____
_____
_____
_____
_____
_____
_____

Interpretation

_____
_____

Feeling Upon Awakening

_____
_____
_____

Comments

_____
_____
_____

Deam Journal

Date:_____   Time:_____

Thoughts Before Sleep

_____
_____
_____
_____
_____

Emotions Before Sleep

_____

Dream

_____
_____
_____
_____
_____
_____
_____

Interpretation

_____
_____
_____

Feeling Upon Awakening

_____
_____
_____

Comments

_____
_____
_____

Deam Journal

Date:_____   Time:_____

Thoughts Before Sleep

_____
_____
_____
_____
_____

Emotions Before Sleep

_____

Dream

_____
_____
_____
_____
_____
_____
_____
_____

Interpretation

_____
_____
_____

Feeling Upon Awakening

_____
_____
_____

Comments

_____
_____
_____

Deam Journal

Date:_____   Time:_____

Thoughts Before Sleep

Emotions Before Sleep

Dream

Interpretation

Feeling Upon Awakening

Comments

Deam Journal

Date:_____ Time:_____

Thoughts Before Sleep

_____
_____
_____
_____
_____

Emotions Before Sleep

_____

Dream

_____
_____
_____
_____
_____
_____
_____

Interpretation

_____
_____
_____

Feeling Upon Awakening

_____
_____
_____

Comments

_____
_____

Deam Journal

Date:_____   Time:_____

Thoughts Before Sleep

_____
_____
_____
_____
_____

Emotions Before Sleep

_____

Dream

_____
_____
_____
_____
_____
_____
_____

Interpretation

_____
_____

Feeling Upon Awakening

_____
_____
_____

Comments

_____
_____
_____

Deam Journal

Date:_____   Time:_____

Thoughts Before Sleep

_____
_____
_____
_____
_____

Emotions Before Sleep

_____

Dream

_____
_____
_____
_____
_____
_____
_____

Interpretation

_____
_____
_____

Feeling Upon Awakening

_____
_____
_____

Comments

_____
_____
_____

Deam Journal

Date:_____   Time:_____

Thoughts Before Sleep

Emotions Before Sleep

Dream

Interpretation

Feeling Upon Awakening

Comments

Deam Journal

Date:_____   Time:_____

Thoughts Before Sleep

_____
_____
_____
_____
_____
_____

Emotions Before Sleep

_____

Dream

_____
_____
_____
_____
_____
_____
_____
_____

Interpretation

_____
_____
_____

Feeling Upon Awakening

_____
_____
_____

Comments

_____
_____
_____

Deam Journal

Date:_____   Time:_____

Thoughts Before Sleep

_____
_____
_____
_____
_____

Emotions Before Sleep

_____

Dream

_____
_____
_____
_____
_____
_____
_____

Interpretation

_____
_____

Feeling Upon Awakening

_____
_____
_____

Comments

_____
_____
_____

Deam Journal

Date:_____   Time:_____

Thoughts Before Sleep

_____
_____
_____
_____
_____

Emotions Before Sleep

_____

Dream

_____
_____
_____
_____
_____
_____
_____

Interpretation

_____
_____
_____

Feeling Upon Awakening

_____
_____
_____

Comments

_____
_____
_____

Deam Journal

Date:_____   Time:_____

Thoughts Before Sleep

_____
_____
_____
_____
_____

Emotions Before Sleep

_____

Dream

_____
_____
_____
_____
_____
_____
_____
_____

Interpretation

_____
_____
_____

Feeling Upon Awakening

_____
_____
_____

Comments

_____
_____
_____

Deam Journal

Date:_____   Time:_____

Thoughts Before Sleep

_____
_____
_____
_____
_____

Emotions Before Sleep

_____

Dream

_____
_____
_____
_____
_____
_____
_____

Interpretation

_____
_____
_____

Feeling Upon Awakening

_____
_____
_____

Comments

_____
_____
_____

Deam Journal

Date:_____   Time:_____

Thoughts Before Sleep

_____
_____
_____
_____
_____

Emotions Before Sleep

_____

Dream

_____
_____
_____
_____
_____
_____
_____
_____

Interpretation

_____
_____
_____

Feeling Upon Awakening

_____
_____
_____

Comments

_____
_____
_____

Dream Journal

Date:_____   Time:_____

Thoughts Before Sleep

_____
_____
_____
_____
_____

Emotions Before Sleep

_____

Dream

_____
_____
_____
_____
_____
_____
_____

Interpretation

_____
_____
_____

Feeling Upon Awakening

_____
_____
_____

Comments

_____
_____
_____

Dream Journal

Date:_____   Time:_____

Thoughts Before Sleep

_____
_____
_____
_____
_____

Emotions Before Sleep

_____

Dream

_____
_____
_____
_____
_____
_____
_____
_____

Interpretation

_____
_____
_____

Feeling Upon Awakening

_____
_____
_____

Comments

_____
_____
_____

Deam Journal

Date:_____   Time:_____

Thoughts Before Sleep

_____
_____
_____
_____
_____

Emotions Before Sleep

_____

Dream

_____
_____
_____
_____
_____
_____
_____

Interpretation

_____
_____
_____

Feeling Upon Awakening

_____
_____
_____

Comments

_____
_____
_____

Deam Journal

Date:_____   Time:_____

Thoughts Before Sleep

_____
_____
_____
_____
_____

Emotions Before Sleep

_____

Dream

_____
_____
_____
_____
_____
_____
_____
_____

Interpretation

_____
_____
_____

Feeling Upon Awakening

_____
_____
_____

Comments

_____
_____
_____

Deam Journal

Date:_____ Time:_____

Thoughts Before Sleep

_____
_____
_____
_____
_____

Emotions Before Sleep

_____

Dream

_____
_____
_____
_____
_____
_____
_____

Interpretation

_____
_____
_____

Feeling Upon Awakening

_____
_____
_____

Comments

_____
_____
_____

Deam Journal

Date:_____   Time:_____

Thoughts Before Sleep

_____
_____
_____
_____
_____

Emotions Before Sleep

_____

Dream

_____
_____
_____
_____
_____
_____
_____

Interpretation

_____
_____

Feeling Upon Awakening

_____
_____
_____

Comments

_____
_____

Deam Journal

Date:_____   Time:_____

Thoughts Before Sleep

_____
_____
_____
_____
_____

Emotions Before Sleep

_____

Dream

_____
_____
_____
_____
_____
_____
_____
_____

Interpretation

_____
_____
_____

Feeling Upon Awakening

_____
_____
_____

Comments

_____
_____
_____

Deam Journal

Date:_____   Time:_____

Thoughts Before Sleep

Emotions Before Sleep

Dream

Interpretation

Feeling Upon Awakening

Comments

Deam Journal

Date:_____   Time:_____

Thoughts Before Sleep

_____
_____
_____
_____
_____

Emotions Before Sleep

_____

Dream

_____
_____
_____
_____
_____
_____
_____

Interpretation

_____
_____
_____

Feeling Upon Awakening

_____
_____
_____

Comments

_____
_____

Deam Journal

Date:_____   Time:_____

Thoughts Before Sleep

_____
_____
_____
_____
_____

Emotions Before Sleep

_____

Dream

_____
_____
_____
_____
_____
_____
_____
_____

Interpretation

_____
_____

Feeling Upon Awakening

_____
_____
_____

Comments

_____
_____

Dream Journal

Date:_____   Time:_____

Thoughts Before Sleep

_____
_____
_____
_____
_____

Emotions Before Sleep

_____

Dream

_____
_____
_____
_____
_____
_____
_____

Interpretation

_____
_____
_____

Feeling Upon Awakening

_____
_____
_____

Comments

_____
_____
_____

Deam Journal

Date:_____   Time:_____

Thoughts Before Sleep

_____
_____
_____
_____
_____

Emotions Before Sleep

_____

Dream

_____
_____
_____
_____
_____
_____
_____

Interpretation

_____
_____

Feeling Upon Awakening

_____
_____
_____

Comments

_____
_____
_____

Deam Journal

Date:_____ Time:_____

Thoughts Before Sleep

_____
_____
_____
_____
_____

Emotions Before Sleep

_____

Dream

_____
_____
_____
_____
_____
_____
_____

Interpretation

_____
_____
_____

Feeling Upon Awakening

_____
_____
_____

Comments

_____
_____
_____

Deam Journal

Date:_____   Time:_____

Thoughts Before Sleep

_____
_____
_____
_____
_____

Emotions Before Sleep

_____

Dream

_____
_____
_____
_____
_____
_____
_____

Interpretation

_____
_____
_____

Feeling Upon Awakening

_____
_____
_____

Comments

_____
_____

Deam Journal

Date:_____   Time:_____

Thoughts Before Sleep

_____
_____
_____
_____
_____

Emotions Before Sleep

_____

Dream

_____
_____
_____
_____
_____
_____
_____

Interpretation

_____
_____
_____

Feeling Upon Awakening

_____
_____
_____

Comments

_____
_____
_____

Deam Journal

Date:_____   Time:_____

Thoughts Before Sleep

Emotions Before Sleep

Dream

Interpretation

Feeling Upon Awakening

Comments

Deam Journal

Date:_____ Time:_____

Thoughts Before Sleep

_____
_____
_____
_____
_____

Emotions Before Sleep

_____

Dream

_____
_____
_____
_____
_____
_____
_____
_____

Interpretation

_____
_____
_____

Feeling Upon Awakening

_____
_____
_____

Comments

_____
_____
_____

Deam Journal

Date:_____   Time:_____

Thoughts Before Sleep

_____
_____
_____
_____
_____

Emotions Before Sleep

_____

Dream

_____
_____
_____
_____
_____
_____
_____

Interpretation

_____
_____
_____

Feeling Upon Awakening

_____
_____
_____

Comments

_____
_____
_____

Deam Journal

Date:_____   Time:_____

Thoughts Before Sleep

_____
_____
_____
_____
_____

Emotions Before Sleep

_____

Dream

_____
_____
_____
_____
_____
_____
_____

Interpretation

_____
_____
_____

Feeling Upon Awakening

_____
_____
_____

Comments

_____
_____

Dream Journal

Date:_____   Time:_____

Thoughts Before Sleep

_____
_____
_____
_____
_____

Emotions Before Sleep

_____

Dream

_____
_____
_____
_____
_____
_____
_____

Interpretation

_____
_____

Feeling Upon Awakening

_____
_____
_____

Comments

_____
_____

Deam Journal

Date:_____   Time:_____

Thoughts Before Sleep

Emotions Before Sleep

Dream

Interpretation

Feeling Upon Awakening

Comments

Deam Journal

Date:_____   Time:_____

Thoughts Before Sleep

_____
_____
_____
_____
_____

Emotions Before Sleep

_____

Dream

_____
_____
_____
_____
_____
_____
_____

Interpretation

_____
_____
_____

Feeling Upon Awakening

_____
_____
_____

Comments

_____
_____
_____

www.ingramcontent.com/pod-product-compliance
Lightning Source LLC
Chambersburg PA
CBHW072056280526
45788CB00006B/2302